Be Big

Gavin Sharples

ZEBRA

Contents

For my girls

Madison and Lea

Published by Zebra (an imprint of the Struik
New Holland Group (Pty) Ltd)
PO Box 1144
CAPE TOWN
8000

First edition, first impression June 2000
First edition, second impression October 2000

Managing editor *Nelisiwe Zondi*

Copy editor *Frances Perryer*

Cover designer *Crazy Cats*

Book designer *Crazy Cats*

DTP *B-Complex*

Printed and bound by Trident Press (Pty) Ltd

ISBN 1-86872-325-9

Conversations with Gav

Introduction

On the morning of his first motivational talk ever, Gavin Sharples picked up the phone to tell the marketing director of the corporation that had hired him, that he'd changed his mind. He was cancelling. Never mind that several hundred people were waiting for him in the auditorium, he felt he just couldn't do it. He was terrified, nauseous, and convinced that he was about to make a gigantic fool of himself. So he picked up the phone, but he never dialled.

Instead, he got in his car and drove to the venue. He parked, entered the building and asked the security guard to direct him to the auditorium. The guard stared back blankly and said, 'It's not here.' He'd gone to the wrong place. 'Now I was really convinced I should phone the marketing director and cancel,' recalls Gavin, who began dialling her number. She picked up and said, 'Oh my goodness, I directed you to the wrong place.'

Half an hour late, Gavin found himself standing outside the auditorium, with hundreds of people inside. The marketing director was introducing him. 'I thought, "Am I mad? What insanity led me to believe I can stand up in front of all these people and tell them to change their lives?" Sure, I'd trained and motivated all the staff in the security and insurance businesses I had, and both were great successes, but this was different. This was not my industry and I didn't know any of the people waiting to hear me speak. Then I heard the marketing director announce me . . .'

Gavin does not remember walking onto the stage. 'All I know is that in that moment, something happened to me. I threw out my opening line – I can't even remember what it was now – and everyone went wild. They loved it. When they laughed, cheered and clapped, I knew I had them! And the more I spoke, the more I had them. Minutes into my talk, I turned into this motivational supermonster: I was leaping around, words were rolling off my tongue, I was going *mal*. I was ecstatic because I knew that I had found myself. THIS is where I had always wanted to be.' At some stage of his performance, he caught the marketing director's eye and what did she do? She gave him a big thumbs up.

Since that day, Gavin has not stopped speaking. Today he is a much-loved, stupendously paid, sought-after speaker on the motivational circuit who has delighted and inspired thousands of delegates at conferences and seminars around the country. Which brings us to this book.

'On a daily basis, delegates from every echelon of society ask me several recurring questions about how to be happy, successful and fulfilled. They also frequently ask me to write a book based on the principles, philosophies and premises of my talk called 'The Big Picture'. So here it is. The Big Picture Book.

I decided on a question-and-answer format as it is easy to read. Part 1 is an overview of The Big Picture: it explains why we're not living happy successful lives and, in general, what it takes to do so. In Part 2 we get down to who we are and how we can transform ourselves from fearful, average people into powerful Big people. Part 3 is about action. It offers guidance as to specific Big actions we can take to turn our lives around. Finally, Part 4 is a quick-check summary of Big questions and Big Answers to guide you every day.

As you read this book, I hope that you, the reader, feel that all the questions asked are your questions. I want to conduct a personal dialogue with each and every one of you, in the hope that what I have to say will help you know how unique, special and talented you are. By the end of this book, I want you to be dreaming Big Dreams, taking Big Actions, living Big Lives and celebrating the Big Picture.

It's yours to claim. So do it. Right now!

Part 1

The big picture: What is it?

I believe we are
all born with the
potential to be
superstars.

The big picture: What is it?

I believe we are all born with the
potential to be superstars. We are all born
with the potential to be successful, happy, healthy
and wealthy. We are all born with the potential to
live a life of bliss. But most South Africans between
the ages of 16 and 81 don't understand this. Why?
Because most South Africans between 16 and 81 are
emotionally dead. We've turned into a 'can't complain'
nation. 'How's it going?' we are asked. 'Can't complain.'
'How's the family?' 'Can't complain.' 'How's work?' 'Can't
complain, 'cause who's going to listen?' You see, we've
forgotten that we are born on purpose; that we are born
with unique talents and abilities; that we are born
creative, spontaneous, adventurous, emotional, kind,
playful and loving.

So what happened?

For one thing, we stopped using our creative brain by the
age of seven. Various studies have proved that children
under the age of seven, irrespective of race, creed or colour, use 98% of their creative brain. Cast your mind back
for a moment to age three when you were still a human
being or rather, a human energiser bunny. Can you remember waking up every day and leaping out of bed because
every day was an exciting challenge? You could do anything and be anything. But by the age of seven most
of us have lost this love of life, this spontaneity; most of us have shut the door on our

creative brain. By the time we reach adulthood, the average person uses 2% of his/her creative brain. TWO PER CENT! The handful who use slightly more, go into advertising. They grow ponytails and wear *kak* shirts and the rest of us bow down before them and say, 'Oh guru, show us how to sell our products.'

Where did our creative brain go?

Down the 'can't, mustn't, don't' drain. Down the 'don't expect to make it in Hollywood or anywhere else because life's not like that' drain. By age 16, we have already been told what we can't and mustn't do so many times, we have already resigned ourselves to a life of second-best. From here, the road ahead to adulthood is paved with mediocrity. We no longer believe life can be exciting. We no longer believe in quality of life because we have given up on striving to be quality people with quality ideas who give quality service. We no longer believe in contributing to life. No wonder only 3% of matriculants find work. The rest have already given up because they don't believe in themselves any more.

Brainwashing and programming: the big conspiracy

How did we land up in this miserable condition?

We were brainwashed and labelled. Brainwashing and labels turned us into miserable little people. As you know, South Africa's famous for this.

*The average person uses **2%** of their creative brain.*

Brainwashing and labels, aren't you exaggerating just a tad?

Not at all. We label people so that we can control them. Everyone is limited by their label. The first label you get, often before you are even born, is the boy and girl label. The name you are given generally relates to your gender. So if you're John, it means you're a boy, and if you're Mary, it means you're a girl. This way our parents know how to treat us and they teach us how to walk and talk like a John or a Mary. If you're a John, irrespective of the fact that we're in the twenty-first century, people will still walk up to you if you're crying and say, 'What are you crying for, are you a sissy?' Or if you put on your mother's dress because you want to play-act being mother, but your name is John, when your Mother sees you, instead of being enchanted, she'll be horrified. She'll tell you to take off her clothes straight away and act like a little boy. Of course, if you're Mary, if you climb a tree and play with guns or talk too loud, people will tell you it's not appropriate to behave this way because you're a little lady.

Is that all it takes to strip us of our individuality?

Far from it, that's only the beginning. Now everyone throws in a bit of colour. Our country loves colour. Most countries love colour. So we get labelled. We say, 'You're black, you're white, you're coloured, you're Indian.' Now we're taught to act like our labels. Whites behave like this, blacks behave like that ... and if you don't conform you'll get *klapped* or ostracised. I recently read in a newspaper that a teenage Soweto girl was beaten to death by a group

**Everyone is limited
by their label.**

of black kids because she was 'acting too white'. What was she doing? She was simply attending all her school classes. Her killers considered her desire for good education an attempt not to be black.

Where is this taking us?

Nowhere. I really mean we are going nowhere, maybe backwards. You see, what generally accompanies our programmed distinction between us and them, left and right, black and white, boy and girl, English and Afrikaans, is intolerance, bitterness and eventually hatred. Crowning this path is religion. A lot of people say, 'Hey, you can joke and talk about anything except my religion.' Why? Because religion is where we get really indoctrinated. Each religion teaches that ITS way is THE ONLY WAY and watch out if you don't believe it because you might just get killed in the name of God. Before we know it we're being told how to walk, talk, eat and pray. We're told who to like, hate, mix with and avoid.

But is it wrong to follow one's religion?

I'm not saying it's right or wrong. What I am saying is that when we are told what to do all the time, it strips us of our creative spirit and our freedom of choice. We learn not to tolerate other religions because we're told ours is the only way.

But what if we're not religious or racist? Then what?

Then you're fooling yourself. How can you not be a racist

after having been raised in a racist society? You may try not to practise racism or sexism or any other 'ism', but you can't completely escape. If you believe you've escaped racial, cultural and religious indoctrination, chances are you didn't escape your parents.

How do our parents programme us?

They want us to be functioning, successful human beings so they constantly tell us what we can and can't do. Children hear the words 'no, don't, mustn't, can't' more than any others. They say, 'No, you can't do that because you're too small,' or 'No, you mustn't do that, it's too dangerous.' Their warnings are generally given out of love, but they destroy our spontaneity and our sense of adventure.

But don't parents just want to protect their children?

That's true, but most parents don't think about what they are saying and doing. I've heard parents tell their kids they were a 'mistake'. They're not being malicious; it's just their way of describing that they didn't plan to have you at the time. But imagine being called a MISTAKE! And then parents wonder why their children have problems with self-image. It's the little things they say that stick and damage children. We say 'sticks and stones may break my bones but words can never harm me'. The truth is that words can kill us: they kill our faith in ourselves and they kill our self-confidence.

Think back to when you were a child. Remember when Mommy was busy washing the dishes and you toddled into the kitchen at age three and asked her for a hug. She said, 'Not now, darling, can't you see I'm busy?' On that day you received your first taste of rejection and your first protective crust formed around your personality. A few days later Daddy came home and poured himself a Klippies and Coke and collapsed into the armchair in front of the TV. You were so excited to see him, you leapt up onto his knee and knocked his drink over him by mistake. Without thinking he clipped you on the side of the head and called you a 'stupid, useless brat'. In that moment, another protective crust was added.

You see, sometimes things are said and done to us when our parents aren't thinking. At other times they are said to us more consciously. Ever been told how 'useless' you are? Ever been told, 'Hey, stupid, of all the children in the world God could have given me, how come he gave me you?' Some of us even thought we were genetically faulty when mother said. 'You know, you are thick, just like your father.' And the crusts grow thicker and thicker.

I'm getting depressed. Surely this is the end of the indoctrination line?

Not quite. Let's briefly address the schooling system. At school, we can't move without being told what to do. We even have to cover our books exactly the same way as everyone else, then stick on labels in exactly the same place. They make us line up, they tell us what to write down in our books, what to study, what not to study. This way, every ounce of internal discipline and curiosity gets knocked out of us. Most of us lose the initiative to do things for ourselves or try to do things our own way because when we do, we're told, 'What's wrong with you?' or 'Why can't you be more like the other children in the class?' By the time we get to primary school, we've already experienced over 40 000 reprimands and rejections. No human can take this, so what do we do? We grow thick, invisible crusts right around our individuality, creativity and personality.

What purpose does the crust serve?

It protects us from rejection. It becomes the mask we wear to protect ourselves from the world. It serves as an ever-present reminder that if we don't want to be rejected, we must be invisible and we must fit in. It teaches us not to ask, because if you ask, you'll get *klapped* or rejected. Once we've learnt this, we never change. Even when we become self-supporting adults, we choose not to stand out and make ourselves heard because we might be wrong. We leave decisions to other people, whether it's our boss, our spouse or our government. They come up with the plan and we obey.

What's wrong with letting other people take the lead?

Nothing, unless you want more for yourself and are tired of being told what to do, when to do it and how to do it.

How do other people get to take the lead?

Brainwashing makes us lazy and indecisive. We lose our initiative and our inspiration. We lose the Big Picture. For example, if you are thinking about getting married, both you and your future husband or wife should sit down and discuss the vision or Big Picture you want for your marriage. Right? Things like: you'd both like three kids, you'd both like to raise them in a non-denominational church, you'd like to take camping holidays, she'd like a house at the coast. But most couples don't share the content of their separate Big Pictures, so what happens? One of them lands up living life according to the other's Big Picture. After a while they feel oppressed, frustrated and resentful because they are living someone else's life.

First best is entirely possible

So what are you getting at?

I'm saying, sit up and realise that you are worth so much more than the life you are living now. You are a unique being with 100% potential. You are nobody's stooge. So sit up and realise that first best is entirely possible. No matter what age you might be, first best is waiting for you to dust off that superstar within. First best is the Big Picture. This book is a journey to help you discover *your own* Big Picture.

You say everyone has a Big Picture, but few get it. Why?

Because we cannot see the Big Picture – and most people do not 'get' what they cannot see. The Big Picture is something we *feel* once we understand what our life is all

No matter what age you might be, first best is waiting for you to dust off that superstar within.

about. To get the Big Picture we need to sit down and ask ourselves: Why am I here? What is my purpose? What do I want to do? How do I want to live my life? These are the basic questions of life, but not many people really investigate them, which is why they don't get the Big Picture.

How do I know if I 'get' the Big Picture?

When you get the Big Picture, you get life. You'll know when you've got it because suddenly you'll feel yourself plugged into life and moving in a positive direction. You'll feel excited, positive, powerful and purposeful. You'll know where you are going and what you want. Sadly, if you're like most people, in all likelihood you're not getting the Big Picture, because most of us are so brainwashed and programmed that by the time we finish school, the final nail has sealed the coffin of our unique, creative being.

So now what happens to us?

Well, it goes like this. Let's say you matriculate and you get a fantastic job in this company. You're one of the rare few who are motivated to really try and crack it; you want to learn, apply yourself, get more customers than they've dreamt of, rise up the ladder. You want to be so successful, the rest of the company will be sitting round the camp-fire singing songs about you one day. You want to be a legend. But what happens? You get to work and you want to contribute new ideas and innovate and make a difference. But the first thing your head of department says is: 'I've got 30 years' experience in this job. So don't think you can come in here with your fancy ideas.' My question to this

Why am I here?

Feel yourself plugged into life and moving in a positive direction.

dinosaur is: 'Do you have 30 years' experience or do you have one year's experience that you've repeated 30 times?'

How does this affect my Big Picture?

Experiences like this reaffirm your inability to make a difference. They numb your enthusiasm. Every time someone criticises you for trying or tells you that you are wrong, it adds another layer of crust onto your personality. It makes you smaller and smaller, until you stop dreaming Big dreams, you stop taking Big steps and you stop asking THE BIG QUESTION.

The Big question?

Yes, it's probably the most powerful question in the universe, the one that guarantees you a happy, successful life.

The most powerful question in the universe

This I have to hear. What is the Big question? What is the most powerful question in the universe?

Gav: ARE YOU A GIVER OR A TAKER? It's that simple. Givers are those people who are constantly trying to offer their best, make other people happy, and who give without expecting a return. Takers are what I call 'WDIGs': their first question is 'What do I get?' Takers are those people who tend to bitch about life all the time, who are always demeaning and tearing down everything and everyone around them and who constantly look for faults.

Are you a
giver or a
taker?

How many people are givers and how many are takers?

The majority are takers. It's not our fault. We are programmed to take and to ask 'What's in it for me?' Strikes are a good example. They're always about wanting to work less hours for more money.

Surely it's only natural to want more for ourselves?

Of course it is, but the only sure way to get everything you want in life is to give. If you help enough other people get what they want, your life is going to change. You'll get fame and fortune and love and everything else you ever wanted. Unfortunately, most of us only give when we want something in return. However, if we do anything in order to receive, we're probably not going to receive. True giving is done without expecting anything back.

We should give without expecting anything back?

Absolutely, give without expecting return and whatever you want in life will come to you *when it finds you worthy*. It is an unshakeable law of our universe that the more we give, the more we eventually get back. This wisdom has been around for thousands of years. But what do we do? We continue being takers and believe our lives will change.

Aren't we just creatures of habit?

No, we are insane. The first sign of our insanity is when we do the same thing every day and expect our lives will change. Here in South Africa, we think we can do business and raise our families the same way it's been done for the past 60 years and expect to get fabulous new globally competitive results and functional families. We've been brainwashed and programmed not to change and to resist doing things differently. Then we wonder why our economy is in a mess, why crime is out of control and why our kids are dysfunctional. Einstein said that yesterday's ideas cannot fix the future. Let me ask you this: WHEN WAS THE LAST TIME YOU DID SOMETHING FOR THE FIRST TIME? For a client, colleague, boss, husband, wife, child? What I'm saying is that not only do we not attempt any new stuff – and thereby stretch ourselves – we don't even know what it is we should attempt. In other words, we don't even know what we want in life! How do I know this? Because when I ask most South Africans what they want, they say, 'I don't know.' If *you* don't know what you want, who does? If you don't know what you want, how can God, the universe, your husband, wife, friend or colleague help you get what you want?

But a lot of people believe it's up to God or the universe to reveal what they want. What then?

A lot of people don't want to take responsibility for their own lives, so they dump the responsibility onto God or the universe. Don't get me wrong, I believe in praying to God – and all her assistants – and to the universe for guidance. I want everyone working for me: every prophet, holy man, guru, spiritual leader and saint. Whoever you want working for you is your individual choice. But if you sit back and do nothing in the belief that it's God's duty to do it for you, all you are doing is inviting brainwashing by whichever religious institution it was that convinced you to buy their brand of salvation.

GET BACK YOUR GUTS

Why don't we know what we want in life?

We've lost our guts. We are too afraid to explore and express who we really are and what we really want. For too long we've been told who we are and what we want. Today, women are told to grow up, contribute to the modern household by getting a job, bring in money, come home in the evening, cook and clean or be barefoot and pregnant in the kitchen, a slut in the bedroom and a fantastic mother. And men are told to be strong, work in a thankless job to bring in money because you have to provide, don't cry, don't complain and don't show emotion. Never mind about what you want or dream of, that's the way life is, we're told.

Isn't this image of men and women a little dated?

Sadly, no. Most people still squash themselves into stereotypes in this country. Sure, there is a percentage of more liberated individuals, but most of them are no better off. They are totally confused about what's expected of them and how to divide their lives between work, home and family. Many people have lost their identity as men and women.

What do you mean?

I mean that when men and women try to liberate themselves they generally swing to the opposite extreme to escape the

**We've lost
our guts.**

old stereotypes. Then men obsess about cooking, cleaning, changing nappies and attending pregnancy simulation classes. And women give up having babies and obsess about competing with men in the workplace aggression stakes.

What's wrong with that?

What's wrong with it is that we've swung from one extreme to another. The same applies to parenting. So many parents these days let their children run riot. Why? Because so many of us feel our parents were too strict on us, so we swing the opposite way. We land up not disciplining our kids at all because we don't want to repeat our upbringing. But if you don't discipline your kids, you're going to have huge hassles with them. Children need discipline.

Aren't you contradicting yourself?

Not at all. It's the type of discipline that makes all the difference. We understand discipline as reprimanding, hitting, *klapping*, chastising and belittling. That's not discipline. Discipline is safety. For example, you're not going to drive across a bridge with a 400 metre drop below if the bridge has no barriers. You know it's unsafe. But if the bridge has barriers on either side you won't think twice about crossing it. Children need to feel similar solid barriers in their lives to feel secure. And the barriers need to be consistent. Let me give you an example. You take your child to a restaurant and the child starts running around, screaming and performing. If s/he did this at home, you'd hand out a fresh one. But because you're in public you don't. Why? Because you're worried what people will think of you. The child knows this and runs riot because s/he is testing the barrier. What you're doing is stuffing up the child because your behaviour is inconsistent. The child does not know where the barrier is. Discipline means loving, consistent barriers. We'll deal with this more later on.

Fine, but I need to know how the discipline you're advocating differs from how our parents disciplined us?

It differs enormously because there was very little we were allowed to do. Our parents wanted us to dress, think and act like them. There was a solid barrier all the way around us that said 'no departure from the norm welcome'. What I'm advocating is two barriers protecting the sides of a road that's wide open ahead. I'm saying encourage your children to think and express their individuality but teach them practical discipline and give them barriers for security and guidance. This way you don't raise a monster.

Okay, so what you're saying so far is that I must realise I've been limited and that I must break through old limitations imposed by others out of love, ignorance or social conformity. I also have to give more of myself because that's the only way to get what I want and I need to muster the courage and discipline to break free, get to know me and move on. But isn't there a short cut or secret to make my journey easier and the results come quicker?

Yes, there is! It's called the Big Success formula.

THE BIG SUCCESS FORMULA

What is the Big Success formula?

It has two ingredients: the first is BE YOURSELF. Shakespeare said it best in *Hamlet*: 'Above all, to thine own self be true.' The second ingredient is a formula I invented: E = MC squared. I know a few people mix my formula up with Einstein's. He did coin the formula, but he got the meaning wrong. He said it stood for Energy = Mass x the speed of light squared. That may be good for his field, but doesn't help us at this moment. $E=mc^2$ has a few big meanings. The first is ENTHUSIASM = MAJOR CASH squared. Enthusiasm and a good attitude are contagious. People catch it and want more. You can change your world by being enthusiastic about life. Walk into a room with a miserable face and see what an instant effect it has on everyone in that room. Now walk into the same room with a smile on your face and see what happens. Everyone smiles back. It is almost impossible to stop yourself from smiling when someone smiles at you.

E = MC squared also stands for EXCITEMENT = MAGICAL CONCLUSION squared. Get excited about situations, people, events, products, and you'll inspire others to enjoy, like, attend, buy whatever it is that excites you. Thirdly, it stands for EMPATHY = MANY CLIENTS squared. Show people how much you care before you show them how much you know. Build relationships based on caring for the individual, not just on money or business. E = MC squared also stands for EVERYTHING = MUST CHANGE squared. Creativity, innovation and change are the tools for the future. We have to change our lives daily, grow with technology, re-invent our marketing plans, services, products and business visions. We have to renew our relationships. We have to decide what we want in life and become creators of our own future. Then we'll start LIVING BIG, PLAYING BIG, BEING BIG.

I identify with these equations, but what about the **BE YOURSELF** part of the formula?

The key to Big success and the greatest gift you can give to anyone is to BE YOURSELF. It's been said that we give away three-quarters of ourselves trying to be like other people.

Give me an example of how you, Gav, practise this.

I'm a hugger. I believe real men hug, so instead of shaking hands, I hug. I love giving and receiving hugs. So I hug as many people – male and female – as I can every day.

But hugging isn't everyone's idea of being themselves.

Precisely – and I'm not suggesting everyone should turn into a hugger. What I am advocating is that you start experimenting with what it takes for you to BE YOURSELF.

The more I am me, the more people want me around. People love meeting authentic people. I love meeting authentic people. Not people who try to be different for the sake of being different, I'm talking about real authentic people. People who you can look at and see there's no

E = MC squared.

ENTHUSIASM = MAJOR CASH squared.

EXCITEMENT = **MAGICAL CONCLUSION** squared.

**EMPATHY =
MANY CLIENTS
squared.**

*EVERYTHING =
MUST CHANGE
squared.*

bullshit there. They are who they are. Of course, we all have images: we wear the latest cut in suits, we drive this or that car, we wear our hair a certain way. But that's all window dressing that masks who we really are. What's important is what's inside.

What I can't understand is that if all this knowledge is available to us, why do we continue to accept society's small picture for us?

Because as people, we want to be loved and we want to be liked. So because of these needs we do our best to fit in so that we'll not only be loved and liked, but respected and acknowledged. Those who don't fit in are called weird. I know all about it. As a child I always felt like an outsider because I never fitted in. I never went to the parties on Friday nights and scored chicks or got into fights so that I could tell the guys at school all about it on Monday. I would stand back and look at these people and think, 'That's not where I want to be.' They would look back at me and say, 'You're weird.' All the while I wondered why I didn't want what they wanted. But I just kept following my own path, even though it was a very lonely path. The great news is that not fitting in has been the making of me. Now I'm making a living from not fitting in. In fact, the more I don't fit in these days, the more money people throw at me. The more I don't fit in, the more they want me at their parties. The more I don't think, dress, walk or talk like them, the more they want me around.

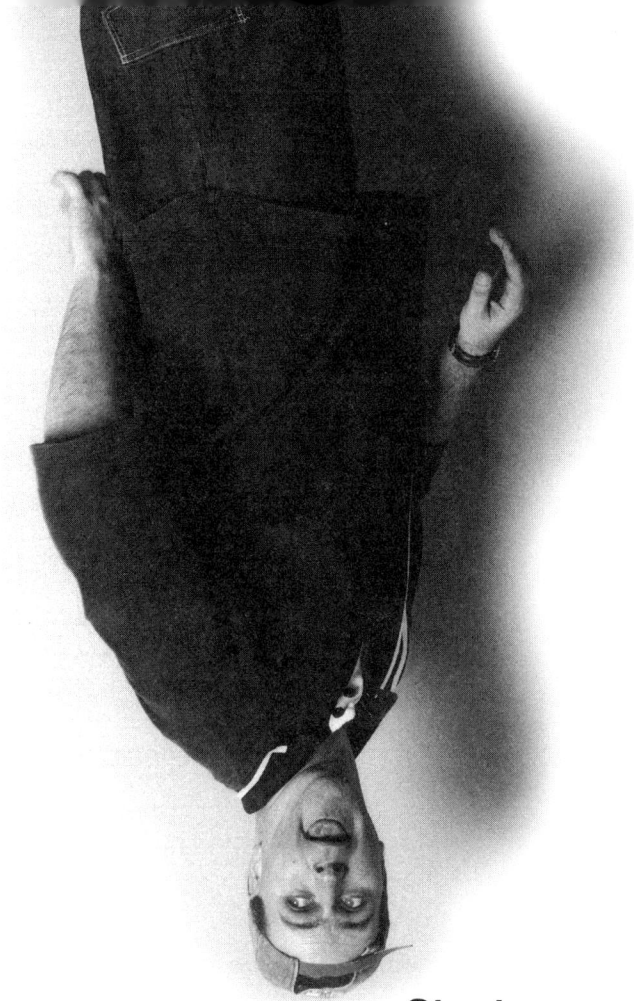

**Start experimenting
with what it takes
for you to BE
YOURSELF.**

EXTREME BALANCE

What else do I need to start discovering my Big Picture?

Whatever we do in our lives, we've got to have balance. Or, as I prefer to put it, EXTREME BALANCE. True happiness only comes to us if we examine and pay attention to every area of our lives and balance our efforts between work, home, money, mind, body and spiritual life, all the time. Remember, we are WHOLE people, and if we have a problem in one area of our lives, it affects all the others. If you're physically unfit or overweight, it will affect your personality, self-image, work, earning ability and personal life. If your finances are in a mess, it will affect your health, job performance, mental health and so on.

Why EXTREME balance?

Balance is for ordinary, average people. Extreme balance is for passionate, enthusiastic, total-commitment people.

How do I apply extreme balance to my life?

Stop being a 'this is how it's always been' person. That's unbalanced because it leaves no room for change. Take annual holidays: do we HAVE to take off four weeks at the end of the year? I know some very successful insurance people who work flat-out for three weeks and then they go on holiday for three weeks. They come back and work flat-out for another three and then they go on holiday again. They do not, as so many people do, work flat-out the whole year and take one month off at the end of it, by which time they're so exhausted it takes them the full month to recover. Far more breaks far more often is one way of applying extreme balance to your life. STOP BEING BLACK AND WHITE. Change old patterns. People are amazed by my lifestyle because their lives are black and white. They say, 'How can you go to the movies at ten in the morning?' Because I can, because I've chosen to live like this. Extreme balance means start living life on your terms. It means choosing new ways of living over old ways to bring balance into your life.

What else do I need to know about extreme balance?

That excess of anything is harmful. We see it with so many movie stars. They seek fame and fortune but when they get it, what happens to many of them? They land up taking drugs or committing suicide. Why? Because they don't know who they are, so they don't know how to handle being a superstar. Too little of everything is also harmful. People who are impoverished or who have no love, also land up with life-threatening problems. I say it again, we have to have balance. This also means we need to accept both good and bad fortune.

Can't we live without bad fortune?

We all dream of living lives in which only good things happen to us but reality is not like this. We're all going to have good and bad experiences. It's part of balance. If you don't know the bad, you're never going to know what good is. Our entire universe works on this principle: it works on good and bad energy, on positive and negative energy.

Isn't it better to try and be mostly positive?

Of course, but it doesn't mean you're going to escape negativity. Positive people in fact attract negativity because it's part of the universal law of balance.

THE POINT OF BEING POSITIVE

What's the point of being positive, then?

It offers us one of life's greatest challenges. If you're a positive person, it's a given that negative people will be attracted to you. But do you allow these negative people to turn you into a negative person, or do you take the reins and see that your positive attitude rubs off on them? The moment you choose the latter, you have started managing your own power. From here you start realising that you have been given the opportunity to bring light into other people's lives. From here you start experiencing the Big Picture.

I'm still sceptical about this positive thinking thing. Isn't it unnatural to force ourselves to be positive all the time?

No forcing required. If you have to force yourself to be positive, you're on the wrong track. If you think that standing in front of the mirror saying, 'I love myself and I'm the greatest' 20 times a day actually turns you into a positive person, you're dreaming. You're falling for the gumpf spoken by motivational evangelists who overdo everything in order to sell books and tapes.

So how do we get positive naturally?

You sit down and ask yourself: What do I want from my life, my work, my family, my body? Then you write it down and START ACTING ON IT. Each step of the way, however big or small, gives you the satisfaction that you are making *your own* Big Dream work for you. From here you naturally feel more positive. But don't panic, we'll learn how to do this further on.

That's great, but what if I don't feel strong enough to handle the negative people I'm attracting right now?

You exercise your power of choice. You choose not to be around them right now. You're not judging them, you're just walking away because they're draining your energy and dragging you down.

EXERCISE YOUR POWER OF CHOICE

But what happens if the energy-drainer is my boss and I can't just walk away?

Firstly, you limit yourself every time you say *I can't.* Secondly, what you do is YOUR CHOICE. If the person is your boss and you think, 'I'd better not walk away because I need this job,' then don't walk away. By choosing to stay, you give yourself the power. Instead of saying, 'I have to,' say, 'I choose to.'

But where's the choice?

Gav: The choice is that YOU and nobody else but YOU accepted the job. If you hate your job but feel you cannot leave, it means YOU CHOOSE to stay and put up with it. You chose your job in the first place and now you choose not to give your boss the big finger. The difference between 'have to' and 'I choose' is vast. If you're unhappy with your boss, choose to discuss it with him/her; alternatively find something more suitable for yourself and choose to move.

That's all very well, but it's not so easy to move on when my job covers the bills at the end of the month.

That's what JOB stands for: Just Over Broke. And about those bills ... you choose a certain lifestyle, so you choose your bills.

Be that as it may, how can I improve my situation?

STOP WIMPING OUT! TAKE CONTROL! Stop expecting somebody else to come along and solve your problems. No knight on a white horse is going to appear and challenge your boss, that's Disneyland. In the real world it's up to us, we are in charge of our own lives, we are our own knight, our own white horse and more. Much, much more. The Bible says God made us in his own image. This means God looked at himself and thought, 'I'm going to make a person like me.' Then God went ahead and made you. What this means is that we have all the talents and gifts God gave us, right inside us. All we have to do is to believe in these gifts, to listen to that voice inside that is constantly encouraging us to try out these great talents and gifts. It's the hardest and easiest step in the world.

I'm still not sure I'm getting the Big Picture.

I should think not. Remember the Big Picture is a journey of discovery. So far, we've only just started pushing the boat off the shore.

How do we know if I'm in the right boat?

The day you start asking yourself, 'What do I want from life? Am I happy with my life? Am I happy in my relationship? Do I enjoy waking up every morning and going to work?' A straight 'yes' or 'no' will do for now. Don't worry if it's no. You can change your life around, starting now. All we need is the desire to look inside ourselves and everything will follow.

Why, what's inside of us?

Inside us all is that superstar who was born to have everything in abundance. Now let's set about achieving this.

Recap:

The big picture: taking steps to achieve it

Realise that you are the product of your conditioning.

Every day, give more than you take.

Take a courageous look at yourself and get to know who YOU are and what you want.

Your attitude is contagious. People catch it from the moment you enter a room, sometimes even before.

Every day, show people you care.

Do something different today, every day.

Look at all the areas of your life and work on them.

CHOOSE YOUR LIFE!

Part 2

Be big, be you

Get a life!

Be big, be you

Okay, so I'm all fired up now to find out who I am and be myself. Where do I begin?

With your past. GET OVER IT. When we are born we are given a rucksack. And God tells us to put all of life's lessons into it but to leave all the pain, hurt, discomfort and suffering outside. But we do the opposite. We pop all our unhappiness, loss and failure in the rucksack and leave the lessons outside. Someone breaks up with you. *Gooi* it in the rucksack. Another deal falls through. *Gooi* it in the rucksack. Your house gets burgled. *Gooi* it in the rucksack. Then I come up to you and ask, 'How's it going?' and you say, 'Bearing up, under the circumstances.' GET A LIFE! Get over it. No matter what Mommy said to you. No matter what Daddy didn't do. No matter what's happened to you, as long as you live in the past, you can never see the future. We are all guilty of living in the past; this whole country lives in the past. We continue to blame everything on apartheid. Why haven't we wiped out crime? Apartheid. Why haven't we tarred the roads? Apartheid. How long are we going to blame other people, other governments for things we are now in control of? How long are we going to blame our past relationships, our past bad experiences for our present unhappiness? Get over it. Move on.

Learn the lesson, discard the event

That's easier said than done. How can we simply wipe out our past?

I'm not saying that. I'm saying learn the lessons of the past. Take the rucksack off your back and turn it upside down. Let all the baggage spill out. Take a good look at it. What lesson did the experience teach you? How can that experience serve you today? How can that experience serve others? That's the big question: how can our life's experiences and lessons help others? Explore each and every experience and find the lesson because this is how you will discover your purpose, this is how to discover your Big Picture. Then pop the LESSONS into the rucksack, making sure you leave out the pain and guilt, and move on.

How can my experience help others?

Let me ask you a question. What sort of person makes the best rape counsellor?

A rape victim!

Yes, someone who has been raped. Why? Because they have the empathy and experience to help someone else in that position. So next time something BAD happens again, use the knowledge you've gained from the event and store the knowledge to serve you and others.

Live 'because of' not 'in spite of'

Can you give me an example of someone who has risen above his/her past?

There are thousands of examples. Take my dear friend Alison: the woman from Port Elizabeth who was kidnapped, raped, strangled and stabbed, then abandoned in the bushes and left for dead. She could have disappeared into some dark hole, but she refused to. She took her experience and said, 'BECAUSE OF what happened to me, I'm living a life I only dreamed about.' I'm flying around the world, helping people, I've published a book and I'm married to a wonderful man. The point is, she didn't say, 'IN SPITE OF' what happened, she said 'BECAUSE OF' what happened.

Victor Vermeulen, the rising-star cricketer who dived into the swimming pool and got paralysed from the neck down, is another example. From the most active, sporting person and a potential Springbok, this young man is now a quadriplegic. He didn't sit back and feel sorry for himself. He used his experience as a platform to motivate and inspire people. He says 'I'm locked in a concrete body but BECAUSE OF it I'm now making a difference to other people's lives.'

What's your story?

But what if nothing like this has ever happened to us?

That's my point. Why wait for something bad to happen to you before you ignite your life. Start living now! Besides, lessons are given to us every day in smaller ways through everything we experience. I get so sick of people asking me, 'So, what's your story?' They want to know what terrible thing happened to me to turn me into a motivator. They want to know whether I had shock therapy or whether I was burnt with cigarettes as a child. We feel people only earn the right to tell their story if they've experienced pain and suffering.

But if you've never experienced hardship, how can you advise people about how to overcome theirs?

I never said I haven't experienced hardship. I have. We all do. The point I'm making is that I don't want to use my sad experiences as a marketing tool to give me credibility. My aim is to help motivate and inspire others because I've discovered tools to help master this life and I want to help you to find happiness. Why? Because I love you. Why? Because I'm a human being and my purpose in life, my Big Picture, is to help others make the most of this precious life.

Fear is your best friend

What is the first step towards making the most of my life?

We have to start chipping through that protective crust that's blocking out your uniqueness and that has turned you into a small person. Chip away at those layers of mediocre thinking that have brainwashed you out of being

Ignite *your* *life.*

a Big Person with a Big Picture. And while you're chipping, ask yourself, 'Do I know what will make me really happy?'

I do, but I am scared to change everything about my life.

I love your honesty. Let's take this slowly and answer bit by bit. First, it's important to look at the words we use, because they are powerful indicators of how we feel. Let's look at 'I am scared'. If you say 'I am', then you make it so. 'I am powerful' is a powerful validation of yourself, while 'I am scared' limits everything about you; it makes you hide behind fear.

Let's look at fear. First we have to realise that fear is good. There can be no courage without fear. We all have times when we are afraid. The difference between courageous people and small-minded sissies is that courageous Big Picture people make changes BECAUSE OF their fear. Fear prepares the body and mind for action. Mentally you become more alert, physically your body releases chemicals to prepare for fight or flight. Any great speaker knows that before any talk, even the ones you've done thousands of times, you feel that nervous energy, that fear we call 'butterflies'. The secret is to get the butterflies to fly in formation.

Now let's look at the words 'change everything about my life'. Why is it all or nothing with people? Who said change *everything*? Change the stuff that's not working for you, keep what is. Acknowledge your positives. Review your life's experiences, find the lessons and start living. Let's stop being sissies.

STOP BEING SISSIES

Why am I and so many South Africans frightened, or 'sissies', as you call us?

It's a little unfair to label people, I know, especially after I've been speaking against labelling. But sometimes the only way to motivate people who function in a 'labelled' world is to give them one to shock them into action. The reason we are scared is because we have a poor self-image. It's so poor that we consider it a victory while driving not to allow someone to slip into the lane ahead of us. Weird! Basically we do not think we are good enough as people. As a country we do not feel we are good enough to compete with the rest of the world. We still think overseas is better, so we try to emulate the Americans. We think so little of our rich African heritage that we have turned into insubstantial American wannabes. We've become small-minded and petty.

How do you differentiate small minds from other minds?

You get three types of minds: small, medium and BIG. Small minds talk about other people: 'Did you hear what Susan did? Do know what Johnny said?' Medium minds talk about business and what's in the news. BIG minds think about concepts, about dreams, visions and goals.

Aren't you born with one or another kind of mind?

The beauty of the Big Picture is that we are all born with and capable of developing great minds, but we have been brainwashed into believing we are not good enough. Given our potential, the question we need to ask ourselves is: Do you WANT a small, medium or BIG MIND? Size does matter. Think big, dream big, live big.

TAKE OFF YOUR MASK

I've decided I want a Big mind, but how do I get one?

Start chipping through that thick, negative crust around your personality, which I call your mask. Why? Because our masks, as the word suggests, conceal who we really are.

Give me an example of the kind of masks we wear.

Many kinds. The largest mask most of us wear is the career mask. When someone asks us who we are, we say, 'I am a doctor, I am a mother, I am a web designer, I am a CEO.' That's not who you are, that's the role you have chosen to play in order to make a living or to identify your functions and other people's expectations of you. It's a mask, a label, a title — and it limits who you are as a whole. We need to understand that the moment we label ourselves, we limit our scope. The word 'wife', for example, limits a woman's experience and expression. We don't think of a business person or a romantic lover or a brilliant intellect when we think 'wife', because the word 'wife' limits our concept of a woman's experience.

How do we know who we really are?

Take off your mask, shed the labels and start focusing on your feelings. What makes you feel strong and happy?

What makes you feel vulnerable and scared? Be open and honest. Because until we have the guts to show people who we really are, we'll never experience our own greatness, our own Big Picture.

Name someone in this country who has shed their mask.

The singer-performer Nataniël. Here's this Afrikaans *boytjie* who hasn't got a problem with his sexuality, who not only proclaimed that he enjoyed wearing make-up and women's clothing but flaunted it in public. He was ridiculed and scorned, but he stuck to being himself and now he's laughing all the way to the bank. Why? Because the more he is himself, the more people want to be around him. Why? Because people love authentic, liberated beings and they want to be around them to see what makes them tick.

Don't you think he's become a parody of himself? That his unmasking has become a new mask?

No, because the thing about Nataniël, Madonna, George Michael and so many of the 'stars' we admire, is that they are dynamic people, continuously growing. But what do most of us do? WE GET STUCK. We find something that works for us, whether it's an image or a business, and then stick to it forever. I say CHANGE! My style right now is the shorts, the tee-shirt and the baseball cap, and I'm going to use it for as long as it serves me. But one day that won't be me any more; then I will present a whole new persona that I'm comfortable with.

Isn't that just another mask?

No, a mask is something you use to conceal yourself when you have no idea who you are. Style is something you use to express yourself when you know who you are. People instinctively know whether you are being authentic or not. That's why you hear people say, 'I like her; she's always herself.' The fact that people comment when someone is authentic, proves it's uncommon.

Why is it uncommon for people to be themselves?

Because, as I said before, we fear we're not good enough or interesting enough to be ourselves. We fear people will reject us if we stand up for who we are. We're used to being what we've been told to be. Take the last elections. I was standing in the voting queue behind this young guy and we got talking. Eventually I asked him who he was voting for and he said the New National Party. When I said, 'May I ask why? What are their policies on crime and the economy? Why are you voting for them?' he looked at me blankly and said, 'Because my father always voted NP.' We follow like sheep because then we don't have to be accountable for our actions. Being accountable scares us. Taking off our masks scares us because it means we have to look at every attitude and opinion we hold and question where we got it from. We have to ask the scary questions like 'What do I really feel?' About God, about abortion, about blacks, about whites, about money, about love, about hate, about what we want out of life ...

People instinctively know whether you are being authentic or not.

KNOW THYSELF

Why is it important to question everything?

Because the most important goal in life is KNOW THY-SELF. If you know yourself, you know your values, and this brings you closer to the real you behind the mask. The moment you start questioning and asking yourself all the scary questions is the moment you take your first step along the road to the Big Picture, to happiness.

How do I begin my scary question list?

It's simple. Get a pen and paper. Now divide the page into three columns. At the top of the first, write WHAT ARE MY VALUES? At the top of the second, write WHAT DO I LIKE? At the top of the third, write WHAT DON'T I LIKE?

Start with your values. Writing down and knowing our values is one of the most important things we can ever do. Values are the basic operating principles that drive purpose. Ask yourself what you feel about the values you have written down. Are they truly your values or were they passed to you by someone else? Do they serve you? Which ones would you like to change? The same goes for the likes and dislikes columns. Maybe you like ice cream and walks on the beach. Maybe you don't like going to gym or art movies. Write down all the people you like and those you don't like. And don't judge yourself. Love yourself for everything you write on the list because you are taking a positive step towards knowing yourself. Now ask your-self which of these likes and dislikes serve you, make you feel positive. Start focusing more on what serves you

Make a *scary question* list.
What are my **values**?
What **do** I like?
What **don't** I like?

and less on what makes you feel bad. We spend so much time trying to fix up our negative sides that we neglect the good in us. Why? Because we're brought up to find faults – ours and other people's – instead of to recognise talents.

But what if the thing that makes me feel really good is money?

There's nothing wrong with feeling good about money. Money is good. Money can relieve a lot of pressure and stress and give you more time to play. Money for money's sake, however, can spell disaster. Happiness cannot be achieved without balance. So we need to find other areas, like relationships or spiritual growth, to balance out our love for money. Which brings me to the next list.

Divide your next page into three again. This time ask questions about three of the most pressing areas in your life: for you this could be work, relationships and money. Write down what you feel about these areas in your life at the moment. Remember this is just for you, so write everything you really feel because this is the moment when you are taking off your mask. This is when you start identifying what you feel, when you start acknowledging your achievements and your mistakes. It's an entirely private matter: all the answers are inside you.

STOP WORKING FOR THE BANK

Say I realise I'm in a financial fix. How do I go about resolving it?

Firstly, stop berating yourself. Now start looking for

solutions. The most liberating and simple answer is: STOP WORKING FOR THE BANK. Between the banks and the advertising agencies, they stop people from liberating themselves. When you ask someone who they work for, they say this company or that company, but the real answer is that they work for the bank. They buy cars they can't afford because the advertisers tell them it makes them look successful or sexy. The advertisers know they've got an ally, namely the banks and financial institutions, who will lend any amount of money for homes, clothing, cars. Before you know it, you're hooked.

How do I know when I'm hooked to the bank?

When you are spending more than you earn and when you are saving nothing. When you believe that it's okay to buy cars, houses and clothes you cannot afford because, as you say, 'It motivates me to work harder and be successful.' You're hooked. Take a look at your pay cheque and see who, after the tax man, is first in line to be paid. The bank. One of the chief causes of divorce is financial problems. The stress and strain gets so out of control that couples fall apart. In fact, one of the reasons people get married is to lighten and share the financial burden. Instead, the expenses increase, especially if you have children. Now you're really hooked because you have a family to support.

What happens to me once I'm hooked to the bank?

You cannot be authentic. You can no longer express what you think and feel. Let's say your boss does something that's unethical and immoral. You cannot speak up. You have to put on a mask of falseness because otherwise you might get fired. Let's say you're selling something that you don't believe benefits anyone. You have to manipulate people into buying it, because you need the money. If you don't, the bank will come and take away the house, the car, the sound system ... all those things you've bought to keep up with the Joneses or the Dlaminis.

STUFF THE JONESES AND STUFF THE DLAMINIS

So what am I supposed to do to get unhooked?

The first thing you have to do is say STUFF THE STUFF, STUFF THE JONESES AND STUFF THE DLAMINIS. Let other people live beyond their income and pretend to be something they aren't, but don't do it yourself. We spend our whole lives accumulating stuff and worrying about who is going to take it away. Get rid of everything that you don't frequently use or need. There's some religion where, every six months, the followers give away everything that's been lying around unused. Imagine that! I say stuff the stuff because it frees you. Now when your boss does something unethical, you can say what you really think because you aren't scared of getting fired. You aren't scared of being honest. You aren't scared of being yourself. And you won't force products on people when they don't need them.

Stuff the stuff.

I say stuff the stuff
because it *frees* you.

It sounds a bit hey-wow-materialism-is-nowhere kind of New Age mumbo-jumbo for me.

Not so, it's totally down-to-earth advice and it applies to every one of us. Most people surround themselves with stuff they cannot afford and it holds them back.

But what's wrong with having nice stuff?

Nothing. I love nice stuff. But get nice stuff WHEN you can afford it. Hold back on the stuff UNTIL you can afford it. Ask yourself, 'Must my shirt really have a crocodile or a penguin on it?' This is mask stuff. We do it because we think it will impress other people. I'm saying chip away the conditioning that makes us believe life depends on the labels we buy, the suburbs we live in and the places we're seen at. It's time to see through this programming. It's time to simplify our lives.

IT'S TIME TO SIMPLIFY OUR LIVES

How do I know what I should be spending?

It's so simple. SPEND LESS THAN YOU EARN. It's a pearl of wisdom, but very few people follow it. Ask yourself, 'Do I have enough money to live on for six months without working?' If you don't, you're overspending.

How do I increase my income so that I have more to spend?

You mean 'to invest'. There's an old eastern proverb that states if you want to get across the river, you sometimes have to take a step or two back to give yourself the momentum to leap. If you want to earn more money, cut back your expenses and start living a more modest lifestyle to give yourself breathing time to work out what you want. Maybe you want to work for yourself, to become an entrepreneur. Take two steps back to leap forward.

I'm not sure I understand how this will help me get ahead.

Let me give you an example from my own life. Some years ago when I was an insurance broker, I decided to get out of insurance and start a security business with some friends of mine. In order to generate leads, we had to do marketing. I decided the best approach was to put on a security guard's uniform, stand at robots and hand out pamphlets. So I did that. On one of these marketing drives, a guy pulled up in his BMW and looked at me through his designer shades. Then he looked at the girlfriend sitting next to him, all done up and looking wonderful. I knew what he was saying: 'I went to school with this oke. Look at him. What a loser.' Then he turned to me and said, 'So how's it going, Gav?' in this condescending tone. But you know what? I knew that his car was bought on credit, that he was slaving away for a boss to be able to cover his expenses each month-end. I knew his chick was probably only with him because of the flashy image he was projecting. I also knew that my security business would one day grow into something Big and that even though I was standing at a robot handing out pamphlets, I was my own boss. Three years later his car was repossessed and he was struggling to make ends meet selling timeshare. Three years later I was driving down the road in my fully paid-for car and I had sold my security business for a gorgeous sum. The point to this story is that I had to take a few steps back. I had to eat humble pie and live with less, but I had a dream to be free. And it paid off big time.

But what if I'm happy working for someone else and I'm in a secure, top-earning job? Why should I reduce my expenses?

No matter how much money you are making, no matter how secure you think your job is, you have to spend less than you earn. You have to ask yourself, 'Is my car, my house, any of my accounts, a millstone round my neck?' If they are, you need to think about selling up and living more modestly. A couple of years ago I was here. I put my house and car on the market. Even though it meant a loss on both, my debt to the bank had to be considerably reduced. Why? Because I had gotten in over my head. We need to think about where we are right now. If it's not a good place, do something about it.

TAKE BABY STEPS FORWARD

Most people can't change their lives overnight. So where do we begin?

I'm not asking or advising anyone to change overnight, unless you are in life-threatening danger. Start by taking 'baby steps'. Identify areas that are not making you happy and start changing things. The first step for most people is to start paying off your debts and stop buying on credit. Keep a jar at home and every night empty your change into it. At the end of the month you pay this into your credit card over and above your normal payment. That is a baby step. Most people say, 'That's not going to help, I'm thousands overdrawn.' But it does help; it makes you aware of every cent you spend.

Okay, so we've looked at work and money, what about relationships? What do we do if things aren't going well?

First ask whether you're in the relationship to take or to give. Next, DO SOMETHING ABOUT YOUR RELATIONSHIP. The majority of people spend their lives moaning about how bad their relationship is, instead of DOING something about it. Do whatever it takes, even if it means moving on.

What steps can I take to sort out my relationship?

Try being honest with your partner. Try sharing how you really feel. Most couples stop sharing the deep stuff after they've been together a while. In the beginning it was nothing but in-depth discussions until the sun came up. The phone bills were unbelievable because we communicated so well during the courting phase. Then we stopped sharing. We stopped sharing our thoughts and feelings and started hiding behind our masks. We stopped being honest. What we need to do now is go to our partner and say, 'We've worn masks for too long. I want to change things. I want us to get to know each other. I want to discover the real you.'

What if, after taking a good look at myself, I feel I've wronged my partner. Do I tell him/her?

Once you do this, you're really moving forward because the hardest task for most of us is to admit we've been wrong. We'll fight it, excuse it, justify it and deny it because not only do we find it difficult to say sorry, but we convince ourselves our partner will never let us live it down if we admit we've been wrong. We convince ourselves it's no use dropping our mask. Most couples in this country never drop their masks. That's why we've got the highest divorce rate in the world.

What you are saying is I have to take off my own mask irrespective of what my partner's response will be?

Right. And if your first attempt at communication doesn't work, try again. But don't set out with the premise, 'What happens if it doesn't work?' Try it before you negate it. And if your approach doesn't work, then don't turn around and say 'I told you so' and give up. Try another approach. Success is not gained overnight. Like a woodpecker, you have to keep chipping away.

But what if my partner, after months of chipping away, still doesn't want to communicate?

If you are truthful with yourself, you will know the answers. I've had to end relationships with women I loved dearly, but I had to acknowledge that we had grown apart. Some of the changes we make are tough. Many

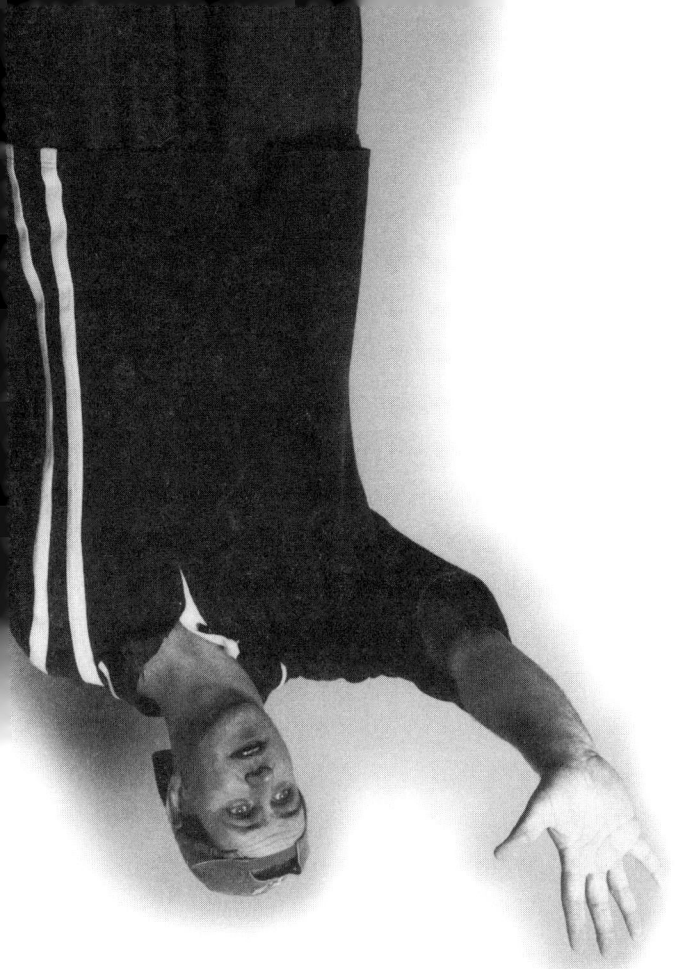

We convince ourselves it's no use dropping our mask.

women in this country have to sit up and acknowledge they are in an abusive relationship. They have to decide what to do about it. The first step is to get out or seek help; there are many organisations they can turn to. I say it again and again, we have to start being honest and take whatever action is necessary to start loving ourselves. If we stay, it's because we want to stay.

Who would want to stay in an abusive relationship?

Many people choose to stay in abusive relationships. I met a woman who says her husband verbally abuses her every day, but that she enjoys the jet-setting lifestyle he provides, so she's chosen to put up with the abuse. That's her choice.

If I've never thought I'm good enough to expect the best, how do I change this?

CHANGE YOUR 'THOUGHT'. YOU ARE A MULTI-MILLION DOLLAR PERSON.

Start realising from this moment on that YOU ARE UNIQUE AND SPECIAL and that you do deserve the best. Let me help you. If I offered you two million dollars right now for both of your eyes, would you say yes?

No.

Okay, if I offered you a million dollars for a leg?

No ways.

How about half a million for an arm or one hundred thousand for a hand?

You are a *multi-million dollar* person. You are *unique* and *special*.

No amount would be high enough.

So what you are saying is that you are a multi-million dollar person who wouldn't sell any part of your body for any amount. Yet you run yourself down on a daily basis. You say, 'I'm too fat, I'm not clever enough, I'm not successful enough.' You also run down other multi-million dollar people: you look at Joe Dlamini and you say, 'He's ugly, he's weird, he's stupid.' I say stop right now! Stop looking at what's wrong with other people and start finding what's right with them. Do the same for yourself. The next time you have a fat attack or a bad hair day, stop and remind yourself that you are a multi-million dollar person. Now start walking and talking and acting that way. You are worth so much! More than you've ever been told you are.

I get your point, but when it gets down to day-to-day living we don't feel perfect. How do we handle feeling imperfect?

How can you be imperfect if you were made in God's own image by God herself?

What if I don't believe in God?

If you don't believe in a supreme being, everything I'm telling you still applies because you are still a unique being. There isn't anyone like you. And as a unique being, you are in charge of your life, so claim your power and start living Big.

You are
worth more
than you've
ever been
told.

LIVING BIG

What can I do to live Big?

Stop worrying about what other people will think of you, because they don't really care. If you took your top off now and ran around the shopping mall, you might cause a stir for the next couple of minutes, but then everyone will forget about you. Take a risk. Ask that handsome guy out for coffee. SO WHAT if he says no! SO WHAT if I go up to Cindy Crawford and say, 'Hey Cindy, will you go to dinner with me?' and she says 'No'? I'd rather be burnt by Cindy Crawford than Cindy van Tonder.

But that's rejection and people hate being rejected.

Precisely. That's why I'm appealing to you to stop not living your life because you fear rejection. You get sales people driving past places where they should call in, but they don't because they're scared of being rejected. SO WHAT if they say 'No'. You're not going to melt. We're all living in these balloons called ego and we think that if someone says 'No', we're going to pop. But if you're a self-actualised person, rejection won't worry you. You won't worry about what other people think, you won't worry if they turn you down. Why? Because you know who you are. And you'd like their company, but don't NEED their company. Feel the difference?

What is the first step to becoming self-actualised?

KNOW YOUR ACTUAL SELF. I'm repeating myself, but sometimes you have to, for the penny to drop. Be clear about who you are and what you think, based on your own experiences and research, not on what you've been told. Be honest with yourself and others. So few people these days live truthfully. Start telling the truth. Remember, the truth WILL set you free. Stop living little lies, stop making excuses, stop avoiding the truth and start the journey of self-discovery.

DREAM BIG

I need practical advice. What can I do to get ahead?

Start writing your dream list. And aim high. Take money: most people want to have money. But when I ask them how much they want, they say 'a lot'. That's not an amount, I want you to write down an actual amount, whatever it is. Five million dollars? Ten million? After that I want you to write down whatever else you want, however outrageous. Write it all down. It's not for anyone else's eyes, so don't hold back.

I'm listening, but did YOU write a dream list?

I wrote mine when I was 23 and a single guy living in a little flat in Rosettenville, working as a rep at Tedelex. I went to the CNA and bought a hard-cover book and drilled a hole through it for a padlock, so that no one else could read it. Then I wrote down my dream list, or 'goal-setting' list as it was called then. I wrote that I wanted to play football for Manchester United, that I wanted to make five million dollars, that I wanted to be a motivational speaker instructing the country's top corporates ... the list went on and on. After a year I looked at my list and hadn't achieved even half a percentage of it. Three years went by and I still hadn't achieved what I was supposed to. I never looked at it again until a few months ago, ten years later. Do you know I had achieved almost everything I had set out to achieve. No Manchester United for me, but the rest ... I was astonished ... right down to the woman I married and the dream house I'm now living in, I achieved. Do you know how scary that is!

That's amazing, but is there anything I can do to start feeling good about myself as I am right now?

You should already be feeling good about yourself by now, because you should have started the lists I suggested. But to give yourself a turbo-boost, get a tape recorder and record all your strong points and all the successes you've achieved from before you started school up until today. Include every compliment you've received. Play it back to yourself once a day. Next, stop comparing yourself to others. Start competing with yourself. We're taught that the only way to be successful is to beat other people. It's negative because you're comparing yourself to other people. You're living your life according to the Joneses again. Rather focus on self-improvement. Focus on the positive. Focus on the fact that you've got a wonderful home and a wonderful family. The other day I looked up from the breakfast table and the maid was singing in the kitchen, my little daughter was riding her bicycle and my wonderful wife was nursing our new baby. I thought, 'Can it get better than this? If it can ... WOW!' True happiness can be found in every second of the day if we just look for it. Happiness can be found in a stranger opening the door for you or someone telling you you're gorgeous. But what do most women say when a man whistles at them: 'How sexist.' Do you know how many women don't get a whistle or a second glance? You see, life is all about perception. And we have the choice to see the positive or the negative. So start seeing the good in everything around you, in your work, your home and yourself.

Recap:

Be big, be you

Get over your past and use the lessons.

Stop using your past as an excuse for not being happy and successful.

Thank your past and all its players for all your experiences and lessons.

Get over your past by using its lessons to guide you and to help others to learn from your lessons.

The tougher your past has been, the wiser you are and the more you can serve others and become extremely successful.

Don't wait to live Big, don't wait for a Big tragedy. Live Big today.

Love your fears. They guide and prepare you for a Big life.

Focus on your strengths and gently work on your weakness.

Stop being a sissy and do something BECAUSE you fear it. THIS is courage.

Take off your mask and reveal the real you.

Please change! Take baby steps, but change everything in your life that doesn't serve you.

Know your values and live them.

Know yourself, your likes and dislikes, in all areas of your life to create balance.

Stop working for the bank. Stuff the Joneses and the Dlaminis.

Simplify.

Persist. Life is a beautiful journey IF lived originally by an original.

Know what you want, write it down and move towards it.

Part 3

Big action

**Get
obsessed
and
enthusiastic.**

Big action

Do you want to know the secret to success and happiness? I call it the Big Secret.

Of course I want to know the Big Secret. What is it?

ACTION. That's the Big Secret. The difference between
successful, happy people and unsuccessful, unhappy people
is one very simple thing: ACTION. The successful, happy
people are the ones who are doing something about their
lives. They're asking the questions and making the changes.
The unsuccessful, unhappy people are the ones sitting
around talking instead of doing. The unsuccessful, unhappy
people are the ones who will read this book and think
their life is going to change without them putting in the
slightest effort. That's what most of us do. That's why I
really believe motivational speakers are a waste of time and
money. We go out, we speak to thousands of people, we give
them pearls of wisdom that guarantee success and happiness,
but when we see them six months later, what have they done?
Nothing. They can't even remember the contents of the talk.
Which says one thing to me: they don't really want to be happy
and successful.

Well, I really want to be happy and successful. How do I start changing my life?

GET OBSESSED AND ENTHUSIASTIC. Get obsessed
and enthusiastic about everything you do from
the moment you wake up until you go to

sleep. Even then, get obsessed and enthusiastic about your dreams. If you're a motivational speaker, study all the motivational speakers in the world, examine their techniques, continuously develop your own and make sure you become the best. The best insurance salesmen, doctors, teachers, secretaries, are the ones who are obsessed with what they do. When people ask them what they do, they don't say, '*Ag*, I've got a boring job.' They excite people with what they do. They SUCK THE MARROW OUT OF LIFE. They're passionate about life!

We all need to be passionate about everything in our lives: our relationship, our sex life, our kids, and our leisure time. When last did you pick up the phone during the day and tell your husband you want him, then put down the phone? He won't be able to concentrate on his work after that. He'll be obsessed with coming home. But very few people make the effort; then they complain about not having a great sex life. Well, hello, you can't have a great anything if you're not enthusiastic.

What's the big deal about enthusiasm?

Enthusiasm is life's biggest turn-on. There is nothing sexier than enthusiasm. You can be any shape or size, if you have enthusiasm, people will be attracted to you.

Get up and make it happen

I want to be passionate, obsessed and enthusiastic. But where do I begin?

Get off your backside and start doing whatever it is you've always wanted to do. If you've always wanted to write a

Enthusiasm is life's biggest turn-on.

novel, start writing a novel; if you've always wanted to get fit, start getting fit. Take that first step. There's an old saying which is so true: the toughest step in any journey is the first one. So take that first step, even if it's a baby step, because that's when you start the momentum.

What could the first step be?

Let's say you want to write a novel. The first step would be to sit down in front of your PC and type the first page. As soon as you've done that, momentum kicks in. Now maintain the momentum: make sure you write a page every day. By the end of one year, you will have 365 pages. It doesn't matter whether you think they are good or bad, what matters is that you take action. Refining comes with repetition. In fact, if you want to change anything in your life, just dedicate one hour a day, six days a week to it. Whether you focus on fitness or better financial planning or a good relationship with your children, one hour is what it takes. And nothing must come in the way of that hour. In no time you'll see amazing improvements. So choose your goal and start today! Now! As Gloria Estefan says, 'Get up and make it happen.'

Love over fear

Why do so many of us resist action if that's what it takes to make us happy. Are we THAT lazy?

No, most of us are THAT scared. The root cause of being ineffective is fear. We operate according to two primary emotions: love and fear. Starting to act on your life means choosing love over fear. It means erasing this block in our brains that says, 'What if I fail?' I believe the only people that fail are the ones who don't try. They sit on their backsides for 40 years and then they say, 'I should have, I would have, I could have.' But the people who play the game of life, they cannot fail. Yes, you might start a company and it flops. So what? Did you fail? No, you just didn't get the result you wanted. So look at what happened, work on your weak points and get out there and play the game again.

Why are we so fearful?

Because that's the way we've been programmed. As I've said before, when we were three or four years old, we didn't know fear. We used to run around and discover new things. We used to be joyous and adventurous and love life. That's the Big Picture and we knew it instinctively. But by about age seven we were told to grow up. We were told 'this is childish' and 'that's inappropriate' and that we must walk and talk and act like everyone else or we won't be loved and accepted. So we got scared. Because we want to be loved. So we started doing what we were told to do for fear of not being loved. Are you with me? Are you ready to let go of fear?

Pretty much so, but what's the next step?

KICK THE BUCKET. A 14-year-old boy taught me this. He said to me one day, 'I can prove to you that, no matter how important people think they are, nobody is indispensable and nobody really makes a difference to their work environment.' I said, 'Go ahead.' He fetched a bucket filled with water and said, 'Stick your hand in here. Now pull it out again. The hole that's left behind is how important you are and how much of a difference you'll make to your corporation.' I tried it and no matter how fast or slow I pulled my hand out of the water, it closed up behind me. This really depressed me. I felt insignificant. Then I realised he was right. If I was only prepared to put my arm in the bucket, I would never make a difference. But what if I was to climb into the bucket, grab it by the rim and start hopping around with it? What if I hopped and skipped and jumped and did somersaults in it? What if I then climbed out of the bucket? What's left now? No water and not much of the bucket. This way, there's no way I'm dispensable, because when I leave, I've kicked the bucket.

I'm not sure I understand.

The point is: LET GO OF FEAR. NOW! THIS INSTANT! Crack open that protective crust and jump around. You'll make such an impact that no one can forget you. But what do most people do? They tip their pinkie in the bucket of achievement to check what the water's like. No wonder when they leave, nobody notices they've gone. Why? Because they didn't realise they were there in the first place. So get passionate, get obsessed and get noticed!

How do I apply passion and obsession to my job?

No matter whether you've worked there for five years or if this is your first day, today when you enter the office, make a commitment that while you are at work, you are

So get **passionate,**
get **obsessed** *and get* **noticed!**

going to give everything you've got to the company or whoever you work for. If you are your own boss, then give 100% commitment to yourself. No half-measures. Commitment is crucial to success. Whatever you do, commit yourself to being the best you can at it. Remember, this applies to all aspects of your life: your health, your family, your spiritual life. Get 100% passionate. Kick the bucket!

Everything must change

We've been apathetic for too long, that's why we live mediocre lives. But the choice is up to us whether we want to lead a mediocre life or an exciting, stimulating, happy, rewarding one.

I'll go for the exciting, stimulating, happy, rewarding life.

The question is, DO YOU WANT IT? DO YOU REALLY, REALLY WANT IT?

Yes, I really, really want it. Now what?

Now I'll give you the Big Answer. Stop searching for the easy way out. Start putting in the hours, start studying, start putting effort into your health and relationship, start sorting out your finances. Work out what it is you really, really want from your life and take persistent actions towards it. Life has a way of giving you what you want when you put your heart, mind and effort into it. Funny things start happening; doors start opening; the right people

Do you want it? Do you really, really want it?

appear. That cocktail party you were dreading attending becomes the turning point in your life because the person you needed to meet is there. Nothing in life is a coincidence. When you know what you really, really want, you start living the Big Picture. I was on a plane recently and I got talking to the woman next to me. Most people spend hours sitting next to each other and don't say a word. In fact most people just silently complain, 'Why do I always get the fat guy?' Anyway, there I was, thinking Big picture thoughts: 'Why this woman, why next to me, how can I serve her, how can she help me live my Big Picture?' She turned out to be some big shot in an organisation and I told her I was a hitman going to do a job in Jo'burg. Somehow we got onto the subject of business strategies. She said she was about to have a company conference and she was looking for this outrageous motivational speaker to open it. She said he wears shorts and a baseball cap backwards. She added that he's apparently very expensive, but apparently he's worth it. At which point I turned to her and said, 'Hi, I'm Gavin Sharples, I'm the guy you're looking for.' A week later I got a call from her secretary to book me. THAT'S what happens all the time when you start acting on your dreams and stop sitting on your potential.

Is getting what I want from life that simple?

Yup, it's THAT simple. Just be very sure about what you want and be clear about the intention behind it. If the intention is noble and honest and for the betterment of everyone around you, you'll experience enduring happiness and success.

Types of action

I'm motivated to change, but what type of actions must I take?

There are different types of action. There's positive action and there's negative action. A positive action is anything that helps you grow and discover your Big Dream. So if you're a sales person, it means knocking on doors, telephoning potential clients, setting up databases, building relationships with people. Taking control of your finances is a positive action. Selling the house and car you can't afford is a positive action. Losing weight if you're fat is a positive action. Some form of exercise every day is a positive action because if we lose our health, we're in big trouble. I'm not talking about running the Comrades marathon. Walking the dog or playing with the kids is exercise. Even parking a little further away than usual from the entrance to the shopping mall is a start. Trying to eat healthily is a positive action. I'm not telling people to eat grass, roots, berries and twigs; we live in a modern society. Eat what you should eat. Balance your meals. Have a MacDonald's burger now and then if you want one. It's not going to kill you. But don't stuff yourself with burgers and cake, then complain you're fat. Apply balance. Laughing, praising, giving thanks ... they're all positive actions. Even non-actions can be positive. Like pausing in the middle of a frantic day to smell the roses.

What about negative actions?

The negative stuff is everything that pulls you down, that prevents you from discovering the Big Picture. Blaming your parents or your school or your government for your lot in life is a negative action. Slumping on your couch at home complaining about your body while stuffing chips into your mouth is a negative action. Practising your mistakes is a negative action. Golfers are notorious in this department. They have a problem swing. So instead of going to a professional to correct it, they go to the driving range and practise the problem swing for several hours. Then they wonder why they're still hitting the ball so badly. People think practice makes perfect. It's not so. Practice makes permanent. Positive practice makes perfect.

So we've got to make sure that we are doing the right thing to get the desired results. Being mean to other people is a negative action. Have you noticed when somebody successful or good-looking or popular walks into a room, someone is sure to whisper something derogatory about them? What they are attempting to do is to pull that person down, so they can elevate themselves. You'll hear people say, 'She slept her way to the top.' What they mean is, 'Look down on her, but look up at me, because I didn't sleep my way to the top.' Or anywhere else, for that matter. Making excuses for everything is a negative action. We could go on and on.

Basically it's all common sense. But why is it so difficult to apply what we know?

Because COMMON SENSE IS NOT SO COMMON.

*Common sense
is not so
common.*

I try to take positive action, but somehow I can't keep it going.

Discipline and consistency

This brings us to the two requirements that come with action: discipline and consistency.

Let's start with discipline; something I think we've lost. Be it at work, in relationships, in the way we raise children, in the way we approach finances, discipline has gone out of the window. Why? Because in the old days we used to have too much discipline, so we came to resent it. That discipline was demoralising and degrading. It was negative discipline. The kind of discipline that said, 'If you don't obey us, we'll throw you in jail and pull out your fingernails.' So we turned our backs on discipline. Now, no one is laying down the law any more and crime is totally out of control. Absence of discipline has adverse consequences: it prevents people from living peaceful, harmonious lives.

Basically, what you are saying is that we need to erase negative discipline and introduce positive discipline to all areas of our life. But how do we tell the difference?

Positive discipline comes from within. It's called self-discipline. Negative discipline comes from outside and is imposed on you. The difference between fulfilled and unfulfilled people is self-discipline.

Consistency

Self-discipline and consistency go hand in hand. It's no good smiling and being happy with your customers one day and the next day you're rude. It's no good trying to make things work in your relationship today but tomorrow you give up. The difference between your serve on the tennis court and Steffi Graf's is that you ace your opponent now and then but she does it consistently. Why? Because she woke up at five o'clock in the morning every day for however many years to practise. And on those occasions that she lost a match, she went straight back to the practice court and worked on what she did wrong. That's why she was a world champion. But do we do this? When our relationship is in trouble, do we try to sort out the problem? When we have financial problems, do we address them? We try, then we give up. Another of these wise old sayings states that the line between success and failure is so thin, few people see it. We give up too easily. If we'd taken just one more step, made one more phone call, sent one more fax, maybe that dream deal would have come through.

Love yourself big time

Okay, so now I understand the different types of action, but I need practical guidance to help me take positive action with my career.

No problem, but before we go any further, I want you to understand that from this moment forward you are going to LOVE YOURSELF BIG TIME. No matter what sort of state your life is in right now, love yourself for it. And love yourself for moving forward. Say goodbye to self-doubt, because the second you start doubting yourself, your self-image plummets and you retreat behind your mask. Focus on what you are right now. Focus on the strengths that you have. Are you with me?

Big career action

I'm with you, but I need to know how to get ahead in the corporate workplace.

Now there's a challenge, because most corporations in this country are not interested in people, they're only interested in the bottom-line. Fortunately, there are a handful that are changing; that are acknowledging, 'that the corporation exists because of people'. Seek out the corporations that want to help their people grow. Unfortunately I believe it's the old 80/20 rule: 20% of corporations in this country are genuinely interested in their people.

What's the alternative, because obviously not everybody is able to get into the 20%?

If you believe in yourself you will get into the 20%. Why? Because they are always looking for good people. Good people are hard to come by. If you've got people skills, you're forward thinking, well-balanced, hard-working and passionate about your job, you will find work tomorrow. The point is: BECOME THE BEST YOU CAN BE. If you're a receptionist, be the best receptionist in the country. Take positive action. Go on skills courses, find out what it takes

Love yourself
for moving
forward.

to be the best. If you're a street-sweeper, be the best street-sweeper there is.

What about affirmative action?

Let's demystify this issue of affirmative action: it's important to state that maybe if you're white in this country, at the moment you will have to prove yourself twice as much, but that's good. It gives you an opportunity to excel.

Act now and wait patiently for success

If I apply all the Big Picture principles and positive actions you've told me about, how soon will I get what I want?

Many people think that if they apply themselves today, they must get a reward this afternoon. You're not going to get it. We've become the 'instant generation' — we want instant coffee, instant success, instant sex, but that's not the way the world works. Do something today and you will reap the rewards tomorrow, next week, in a month, in two months or a year. WHATEVER YOU DO TODAY, WILL SERVE YOU IN THE FUTURE. There's an old saying — all the old sayings are so true: all good things come to those who wait. Nothing worth while comes easily. People have to understand that they must be patient with success. It's a process (and when I say success I mean happiness as well), it will eventually work itself out if you take positive action. If you keep chipping away the masks and trying to be both honest and passionate about everything you do, eventually the Big Picture will fall into place. Good guys always come first in the long run. And that's what I say to people – be good guys.

What makes a good guy?

Honesty, integrity, loyalty, not ripping people off, giving more than you take, patience. I know it's not easy. I'm one of those people who gets down on my knees at night and says to God, 'Please give me patience, and hurry.' But patience does comes with practice.

I'm a very impatient person. Give me a practical tip that will help me practise patience.

Go to the supermarket down the road. Next time you want to throttle the person in front of you in the queue – it says baskets only and they are standing there with an overflowing shopping trolley – just stand back and think. Maybe you are being held up for a reason: remember there are no coincidences. Maybe if you'd got out of there faster, you would have been involved in a car accident, and they've stalled you from getting into the car.

What happens if I explode before I think?

That's fine. Once you've exploded, assess the outburst. Don't let any explosion go unchecked. Check why you responded that way. Was it appropriate? How COULD you have reacted? Then forgive yourself and move on.

Make friends with guilt

But what about guilt? When I do something I'm not proud of, I feel flooded with guilt.

That's good. Guilt is a positive emotion. A lot of people think guilt is our enemy. But guilt is our friend because it helps to guide us. Let's say you're in a relationship but you're away from home, alone. You go out and meet this enchanting stranger and next thing you're making whoopee. You have a wonderful evening, the angels weep, the earth moves. Next morning you wake up and you feel guilty. You feel you're a bad, bad person. Yes, you are, you're naughty, noo-noo, don't do this stuff it can only have bad effects, but if you feel guilty, it proves that you're actually a good person.

Only good people feel guilt. Bad people don't feel guilt. Obviously if you're going to go out and do stuff and think that guilt will wash it all away, you're deluding yourself. Eventually you'll stop feeling guilty and become a conscienceless person.

Control your thoughts

What do I do when negative thoughts pop up and try to hamper my Big Actions?

Identify your negative thought pattern. Give it a name. I call it Dave. As soon as Dave comes in whispering 'can't, mustn't', I say, 'Thanks Dave,' and I acknowledge that the thought was there but I don't give it power. And if it comes back, I'll say, 'Listen, Dave, bugger off and find something

Only good people
feel guilt.

positive.' I appreciate that it's very difficult, almost impossible, to control all our thoughts because they're based on our life's experiences. They pop into our heads at the most inconvenient moments and don't easily go away. For example, my thoughts see a child walking along a road; next thing the child is knocked down by a car. If I get caught up in this abstract, negative thought, it will put me right down and make me fearful because I'm a father. So we've got to catch ourselves each time we have a negative thought and show it the door. Then think: 'Okay, what's the opposite of that?' The child can walk down the road and all of a sudden an ice cream truck can stop and give him a big ice cream.

I'm getting closer to experiencing my Big Picture but I'm still plagued by insecurities about myself.

If you have insecurities about yourself, it means you have insecurities about God. What you're saying is: God made a flop here. God made millions and millions of wonderful people, but with me he dropped the ball. I don't think so. God does not make flops. So catch a wake-up. Get a grip.

Ask yourself scary questions every day

I need more practical advice to rise above my insecurities.

Okay, the best way to rise above insecurities is to confront them. Ask yourself the scary questions every day. Like: 'Did I show Dave the door today?'; 'Did I give more than I took?'; 'What do I now know about the world, about me, about people today that I didn't know yesterday?'; 'What did I do for the first time, today?'; 'Did I stretch my talents today?'; 'What did I do that I was actually afraid to do?'; 'Am I living my purpose?'; 'Did I do something today that gets me closer to my Big Picture?'; 'Did I act like the person I want to be today?'; 'Was I patient today?'

I DARE YOU

Believe it or not, I'm starting to get the Big Picture. What can I do right now to take one big step closer to it?

I dare you to walk up to a stranger in the street and pay them a compliment. Tell them they have beautiful eyes, tell them they have a wonderful soul. I met a woman in Cape Town recently who is really the nicest person. So I said to her, 'I would like to become your friend. I would like you to get to know my family and I would like to get to know you because there is something so nice about you.' You know what happened? Tears welled up in her eyes and she said, 'That's the nicest thing anybody has ever said to me.' If you're single, I dare you to walk up to someone you find attractive and ask them out. All you men out there, I dare you to go up to your father and ask if you can give him a hug. All you women out there, I dare you to phone your husband at work and tell him you want him. All you men out there, I dare you to send your wife a big bunch of flowers today and tell her how much you love and appreciate her. All the more if you haven't done this for 20 years. I dare you to go to movies in the morning. I dare you to be the best you can be at everything in your life. I dare you to live passionately. I dare you to be a happy, successful, Big Picture person.

Be a
happy,
successful,
Big
Picture
person.

Recap:

BIG ACTION

Do something, take Action, do it now, do it Big!

Get passionate about everything you do.

Take baby steps, you're on a fantastic journey.

Fear is your friend; it's the seed of courage and the inspiration of heroes.

Get involved, 100% involved; go out and kick the bucket.

Re-invent yourself, your actions, your image, your life.

Be consistent and never stop trying.

Practise internal discipline.

Love your talents and strengths; stop berating yourself for perceived weaknesses.

Start the Big journey today. Act and wait patiently for the floodgates of success to open.

Good people feel guilty. Guilt says, 'Hey! That's not appropriate behaviour. Change!'

Be aware of your negative thoughts and manage them.

I dare you to LIVE BIG!

Part 4

Big questions and big answers

*You can be **happy** most of the time. How?*

Big questions and big answers

Here's a list of questions most commonly asked of Gav. They have all been answered in the first three chapters, but this quick-check summary will help clarify what you need to know.

How can I be happy all the time?

You can't. Anybody who comes into work and is smiling and dialling, circulating and percolating, always up and always positive ... check what they are smoking, snorting or shooting, because as humans we can't be happy every single day. We've got bonds to pay, family pressures, work pressures, people close to us die, we get sad, we've got stuff to deal with. Besides, it would be boring to be happy 24 hours a day; happiness would lose its value. The only way to know happiness is to know sadness. The good news is YOU CAN BE HAPPY MOST OF THE TIME. How? Live life passionately and purposefully. Go out and do good. Find focus in your life. Develop extreme balance – invest equally in your finances, your relationship, your health, your career, your mind, your spirit. Strive for extreme balance every single day and you will be happy most of the time. Take time out to look at the flowers, trees, birds, human beings – all the incredible creations on this planet – and you will be happy most of the time.

How can I live a hassle-free life?

Simple. Don't do anything. Hassles only come when you do something and it doesn't go according to your plan. So don't do anything. Don't phone anybody, don't ask anybody out, don't try a new job, don't take any risks. Just keep to yourself, shut up and mind your own business. Alternatively, get out there and live and don't think of hassles as problems. Rather see them as signposts sent to guide us. When a hassle comes along, it's saying: Change course, change the way you're doing things. It's all about how you choose to see things. Choose not to see hassles as problems, see them as exciting challenges you were sent to solve.

How can I avoid rejection and failure?

Again, don't ask for anything, don't apply for anything, don't start your own company, don't invite him or her out, don't, don't, don't. Simple. However, if you live in the real world, chances are you are not going to be able to totally avoid rejection and failure. What you need to do is stop taking things personally. Nine times out of ten the person who's rejecting your product, service and approach, is not rejecting you as a person. How do I know this? Well, answer this: Does this person know you personally? No. Have they been to your house? No. So how can their rejection be personal? 'But they rejected my sales presentation,' you reply. Yes. So what? Maybe the timing of your proposal wasn't right. There are a thousand different reasons why, but we choose to take it personally. Remember, rejection only becomes rejection when you see it as rejection. Why not rather see rejection as a delayed response for a later confirmation. Fred Astaire did. After his first audition, they sent him a rejection note

See hassles as
exciting challenges
you were sent to
solve.

saying, 'Cannot act, cannot sing, dances a little.' He kept it over his fireplace and as he became more and more famous, he'd look at it and laugh. Do you know the publishers of this very book rejected my first book, saying it was too poor to publish? A few years later I'm approached by them to publish me. Crazy, hey!

How can I make more money?

Do what you love, love what you do. If you chase money, money will elude you. In my life, every job that I went into to pay the bills, I battled. Every venture I've gone into wanting to make a difference in people's lives, has flown. That's why I only take on projects where I know that I can make a difference to others.

How can I become a millionaire?

Get involved in a job that you are passionate about and the money will start chasing you. Invest wisely. Save. Take out some kind of endowment policy or a savings plan. If you want to become a millionaire overnight, find some way to serve your fellow man that nobody else has thought of before. Every one of us comes up with a multi-million dollar idea at some time or another, but we don't action them. How many times haven't we thought up some amazing gadget, only to see it in the shops a short while later. Then we say, 'Hey! That was my idea!' You know Barney, the little purple dinosaur for children? A woman invented Barney because she couldn't find a toy that amused her child enough. So she got some purple material, sewed it up into a creature called Barney and

Every one of us comes up with a multi-million dollar idea at some time or another, but we don't action them.

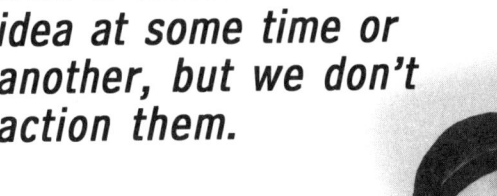

gave it to her child. He loved it. Then some friends saw it and asked if she'd make Barneys for their children. Soon, more and more people started asking for Barney, so she opened up a little business in her garage. Then a big toy manufacturer heard about Barney and the rest is history. Because of Barney, this woman is now a multi-millionaire.

There are endless examples of how people become millionaires overnight. Take the guy who sold short-term insurance and one day he decided he wanted to do it without any physical contact with clients. No physical filling-in of forms. He wanted to phone up clients, sell insurance and substitute written contracts with recorded voice contracts. People said he was mad. Today he's a multi-zillionaire.

Finally, if you want to be a millionaire, don't give up. Most millionaires were bankrupt before they became millionaires. Walt Disney went bankrupt a few times before he hit it Big.

How do I make a million working for a corporation?

You can make a million working for a corporation, no problem, IF you work on commission and you manage your commission. I met a guy in America who sells suits in a department store. He doesn't have shares in the company, he's not a manager, all he does is sell suits for a basic commission. But guess what? He is a millionaire selling suits – he's built up such a reputation that people from all over America fly to San Francisco to be served by him and him alone. Why? Because he gives top, personalised

DON'T give up.

service and he always delivers. He calls people up when new suits he knows they'll like come in. He sends birthday cards, thank-you cards, anniversary cards. He spends an hour every day maintaining contact with his client base. He's become such a legend in the industry that he now writes books on service.

If I downscale my lifestyle, won't people think I'm in trouble?

No, THEY'RE the ones in trouble, because they're still pretending they can afford their lifestyle. And why are you so worried about what people think of you? Because you're still wearing that mask, you're still trying to keep up with the Joneses and the Dlaminis. Take it off!

Should I resign from my job today?

That's stupid and illogical. You've created a world for yourself, and you and your family are living off it. Rather, identify what it is you want from life, then start taking steps to change.

Do you think I should emigrate?

Yes, please! I love it when people emigrate. It's more opportunity for me. Every time someone leaves, they leave their client base behind. I wish more motivational speakers would emigrate: all the more audiences for me. Personally I believe that this country's streets are paved with gold. All we have to do is be 1% better than the average person. That's easy, because the average person does not return phone calls, they do not get things done

I love it when
people emigrate.

on time, they're not prepared to go the extra mile, they're not even prepared to smile at you when you walk through the door. Be 1% better than the average, and you'll reap the gold.

How do I get people to like me?

There are two methods. The first is: Don't be yourself. Be unauthentic. Please everybody. Never argue. Never tell people what you really think. Never stand up for yourself. Become a doormat. However, if you want people to like you for who you are — which brings us to the second method — first like yourself. If you really like yourself and you're your own best friend, it's difficult for other people not to genuinely like you for who you are. Be authentic and you'll attract lots of authentic friends. Be a yes-woman or yes-man, and you'll attract lots of superficial friends.

How can I be more physically attractive to men/women?

Be yourself, be authentic, be proud of you. No matter what size or shape you're in; no matter whether you look like this or that, be proud of you. Let's say you're carrying a bit of extra weight. The worst thing you could do is try and hide it. Why? Because you're pretending to be something that you're not. News flash — I found that in my years of sowing my wild oats, the most attractive women are the ones who are totally at ease with their bodies, irrespective of whether they're a couple of kilos overweight. In fact these women are often the best lovers, because they're not as neurotic as women who obsess about being skinny.

Be authentic and you'll attract lots of authentic friends.

They say, 'This is me, I'm built for comfort, not speed.' Always remember, we need extreme balance. If we focus too much on our physical selves, we might have all the muscles in the right place, but it doesn't mean people will find us attractive. Quite the contrary. There's something off-putting about people who feel they have to put their bodies on display all the time. It's overcompensation. The same goes for people who go out of their way not to take care of their appearance. Something is off balance. To be physically attractive to men/women, simply take the hand of cards God dealt you and play them all to the best of your ability.

How do I meet the man or woman of my dreams?

The man or woman of your dreams hasn't been invented. That's our problem: we set ourselves up for failure. We list several qualities we want. What happens if a man/woman comes along and s/he only has two out of the four must-have qualities? Forget this. Start accepting people for who they are, and loving them for what they are. You'll find it a lot easier to find great men or women. Do you want to meet the person of your dreams? Stop looking. Live your life and a wonderful person will find you.

How do I learn to love myself?

Know that you are perfect because God made you. And God doesn't make any mistakes. Believe in yourself every day and know that you are special. Tell yourself every single day that you are a unique, giving person. Tell yourself, 'I will pass this way but once, therefore any

Live
your
life.

goodness that I can do, I will do now. Because now is my chance to make a difference and to show myself and others that I do make a difference.'

What is my purpose on earth?

To love people around you and to share whatever it is that God gave you. If you understand that principle, your next step is to find out what you are going to do in this lifetime to make people say, 'I'm glad I knew that person.' What are you going to do to help your fellow man? If you figure that out, you're well on your way, because that is when you start living the purpose. You're going to start living the reason why you are here. That's when money and fame and recognition and romance all fall into place.

How did you, Gavin Sharples, become a motivational speaker?

A synchronised event — a coincidence. Years ago I sat down and wrote down a plan for my life. One of the things I wanted to do was teach. I originally thought I wanted to teach school children. After I'd written my goals and planned my life, I just followed where the coincidences led me. One day I went to complain about poor service to the managing director of my cellphone company. He said, 'What do you know? How can you talk with authority about customer service?' And I said, 'Well, I've just sold a very successful business I started and I'm thinking of writing a book on the subject.' So he said, 'Could you put together a lecture on customer service for my company?' I said, 'Why not?' I just decided to go with the flow. I phoned about seven training companies and got prices from them — how much would they charge for X number of people to attend X number of lectures for X number of days. I found the average price. I put together a proposal, and I submitted it to a woman in the marketing division, who was about to move to another company. Guess what? Nothing happened. Absolutely nothing. Never heard another thing from them. But two months later the woman who had now moved to another company, asked me to come and give a motivational talk to her new company and the whole thing started snowballing. I started getting my style and refining the Big Picture message I wanted to share. The rest is history.

How do I know if I've got the Big Picture?

You'll know. You'll feel it. The big picture is in everybody, but if someone still has to spell it out for you, you haven't got it yet. When you get it, you can't explain it to anybody, what you can do is live it. Every single day. Behind every single thing that we do, behind our highest good, behind our highest self, is one thing: LOVE. Love is the Big Picture, the Big Motivator, the Big Purpose and the Big Answer. LOVE!

Love is the Big Picture, the Big Motivator, the Big Purpose and the Big Answer. LOVE!